TAXIDERMY VOL.2
SMALL BIRDS

THE COLLECTION, SKINNING AND MOUNTING OF SMALL BIRDS

BY

VARIOUS AUTHORS

Copyright © 2013 Read Books Ltd.
This book is copyright and may not be
reproduced or copied in any way without
the express permission of the publisher in writing

British Library Cataloguing-in-Publication Data
A catalogue record for this book is available from the
British Library

CONTENTS

TAXIDERMY 1

HISTORY OF TAXIDERMY 5

COLLECTING SKINS OF SMALL BIRDS 9

MOUNTING SMALL BIRDS 56

Other Works in the Series

Birds Vol. 1.

Small Birds Vol. 2.

Fish Vol. 3.

Insects Vol. 4.

Small Mammals Vol. 5.

Large Mammals Vol. 6.

Mammal Heads Vol. 7.

Reptiles Vol. 8.

Bones and Skeletons Vol. 9.

Collecting Specimens Vol. 10.

Skins Vol. 11.

Tanning Vol. 12.

Mounting Vol. 13.

Rugs and Robes Vol. 14.

Taxidermy

Taxidermy (from the Greek for *arrangement of skin*) is the art of preparing, stuffing, and mounting the skins of animals (especially vertebrates) for display (e.g. as hunting trophies) or for other sources of study. Taxidermy can be done on all vertebrate species of animals, including mammals, birds, fish, reptiles, and amphibians. A person who practices taxidermy is called a taxidermist. Taxidermists may practice professionally for museums or as businesses, catering to hunters and fishermen, or as amateurs, such as hobbyists, hunters, and fishermen. To practice taxidermy, one should be very familiar with anatomy, sculpture, and painting, as well as tanning.

The preservation of animal skins has been practiced for a long time. Embalmed animals have even been found with Egyptian mummies. Although embalming incorporates the use of lifelike poses, it is not technically considered taxidermy though. The earliest methods of preservation of birds for natural history cabinets were published in 1748 by the French Academician *Réaumur, and four years later, techniques for* mounting were described by M. B. Stollas. By the eighteenth century, almost every town had a tannery business. In the nineteenth century, hunters began bringing their trophies to upholstery shops, where the upholsterers would actually sew up the animal skins and stuff them with rags and cotton. The term 'stuffing' or a 'stuffed animal' evolved from this crude form of taxidermy. Professional taxidermists prefer the term 'mounting' to 'stuffing' however. More sophisticated cotton-wrapped wire bodies supporting sewn-on cured skins soon followed.

In France, Louis Dufresne, taxidermist at the *Muséum National d'Histoire Naturelle* from 1793, popularized arsenical soap (utilising the chemical Arsenic) in an article titled, *Nouveau Dictionnaire D'Histoire Naturelle* (1803–1804). This technique enabled the museum to build the greatest collection of birds in the world. Dufresne's methods spread to England in the early nineteenth century, where updated and non-toxic methods of preservation were developed by some of the leading naturalists of the day, including Rowland Ward and Montague Brown. Ward established one of the earliest taxidermy firms, Rowland Ward Ltd. of Piccadilly. Nevertheless, the art of taxidermy remained relatively undeveloped, and the specimens that were created remained stiff and unconvincing.

The golden age of taxidermy was during the Victorian era, when mounted animals became a popular part of interior design and decor. For the Great Exhibition of 1851 in London, John Hancock, widely considered the father of modern taxidermy, mounted a series of stuffed birds as an exhibit. They generated much interest among the public and scientists alike, who considered them superior to earlier models and were regarded as the first lifelike and artistic specimens on display. A judge remarked that Hancock's exhibit 'will go far towards raising the art of taxidermy to a level with other arts, which have hitherto held higher pretensions.'

In the early twentieth century, taxidermy was taken forward under the leadership of artists such as Carl Akeley, James L. Clark, Coleman Jonas, Fredrick and William Kaempfer, and Leon Pray. These and other taxidermists developed anatomically accurate figures which incorporated every detail in artistically interesting poses, with mounts in realistic settings and poses. This was quite a change from the caricatures popularly offered as hunting trophies. The methods of taxidermy have substantially improved over the last century, heightening quality and lowering toxicity. The animal is first skinned in a process similar to removing the skin from a chicken prior to cooking. This can be accomplished without opening the body cavity, so the taxidermist usually does not see internal organs or blood. Depending on the type of skin, preserving chemicals are applied or the skin is tanned. It is then either mounted on a mannequin made from wood, wool and wire, or a polyurethane form. Clay is used to install glass eyes, which are either bought or cast by the taxidermist themselves.

As an interesting side note, with the success of taxidermy has come the sub-genre of 'rogue taxidermy'; the creation of stuffed animals which do not have real, live counterparts. They can represent impossible hybrids such as the jackalope and the skvader, extinct species, mythical creatures such as dragons, griffins, unicorns or mermaids, or may be entirely of the maker's imagination. When the platypus was first discovered by Europeans in 1798, and a pelt and sketch were sent to the UK, some thought the animal to be a hoax. It was supposed that a taxidermist had sewn a duck's beak onto the body of a beaver-like animal. George Shaw, who produced the first description of the animal in the *Naturalist's Shunga Miscellany* in 1799, even took a pair of scissors to the dried skin to check for stitches. Today, although a niche craft, the art of taxidermy - rogue or otherwise, is still thriving.

HISTORY OF TAXIDERMY

It is very evident that this art—Taxidermy, preservation or care of skins—had its origin far back before the dawn of written history. There existed then as now the desire to preserve the trophy of the hunter's prowess and skill and the unusual in natural objects.

As far back as five centuries B. C. in the record of the African explorations of Hanno the Carthaginian, an account is given of the discovery of what was evidently the gorilla and the subsequent preservation of their skins, which were, on the return of the voyagers, hung in the temple of Astarte, where they remained until the taking of Carthage in the year 146 B. C.

This, of course, was not the art as we know it now, but shows the beginnings of what might be called the museum idea. The art of embalming as practiced by the ancient Egyptians was, however, effective, not for the purpose of having the specimens look natural, or for exhibition, but to satisfy the superstition of the times, and though a preservative art, hardly to be classed with taxidermy.

In the tombs of that period are found besides the mummies of human beings, countless others of dogs, cats, monkeys, birds, sheep and oxen. There have been a number of efforts made to substitute some form of embalming for present day taxidermy but without much success, for though the body of the specimen may be preserved from decay without removing it from the skin, the subsequent shrinkage and distortion spoil any effect which may have been achieved.

AN EARLY DAY SPECIMEN.

The first attempt at stuffing and mounting birds was said to have been made in Amsterdam in the beginning of the 16th century. The oldest museum specimen in existence, as far as I know, is a rhinoceros in the Royal Museum of Vertebrates in Florence, Italy, said to have been originally mounted in the 16th century.

Probably on account of the necessary knowledge of preservative chemicals, the art seems to have been in the hands of chemists and astrologers, chiefly, during the middle ages, and stuffed animals such as bats, crocodiles, frogs, snakes, lizards, owls, etc., figure in literary descriptions of their abodes. Then as now also, the dining halls of the nobles and wealthy were decorated with heads and horns procured in the hunt.

The first publications on the art seem to have been made in France, in which country and Germany, many still used methods and formulas originated. Though the first volume of instruction in taxidermy was published in the United States as late as 1865, it has been left for the study and ingenuity of American taxidermists to accomplish what is probably work of as high a standard as any in the world.

The Ward establishment at Rochester has turned out many well trained taxidermists, the large museums of the United States are filled with some of the best work of the kind in existence, besides many persons who have engaged in it for commercial purposes or to gratify private tastes. Many of these have made public their methods and modes in various publications. Among these are the works of Batty, Hornaday, Shofeldt, Davie, Rowley, Maynard, Reed and others, all of which are invaluable books of reference for the home taxidermist.

It is to be regretted that the once flourishing Society of American Taxidermists has not been perpetuated, numbering, as it did, among its membership the best artists in their line in this country.

There is no royal road to success in this, more than any other of the arts and sciences, though I believe the ambitious beginner will find the way smoother; better materials are to be had, more helpful publications to be consulted and the lessening supply of wild life tends to make a more appreciative public than ever before.

COLLECTING SKINS OF SMALL BIRDS

THE lives of hundreds of thousands of wild birds have been sacrificed to no purpose by persons claiming to be ornithological collectors, and yet who had not the knowledge, skill, or industry to make up good bird skins. There are now in this country numerous large collections of bird skins that are a sight to behold. The ability to make up fine, clean, shapely, well-preserved skins, and make them rapidly also, is a prime requisite in anyone who aspires to be sent off to interesting "foreign parts" to shoot, collect, and see the world—at the expense of someone else. An aspiring young friend of the writer, whose soul yearned to travel and "collect," missed a fine opportunity to make a very interesting voyage on the *Albatross*, for the sole reason that with all his yearning he could not make good bird skins,—and it served him right for his lack of enterprise.

Let me tell you that, while twenty years ago any sort of a bird skin was acceptable to a museum, now such specimens must be first class in order to be well received. Fine skins are *the rule* now with curators and professional ornithologists, and poor ones the exception. Although the work itself is simple enough, it is no child's play to perform it successfully.

It is best for the beginner to learn first how to skin small birds, and make up their skins, and when he has mastered these details he is prepared to undertake the preparation of large specimens, and learn how to overcome the exceptional difficulties they present. To this end the present chapter will be devoted to setting forth the leading principles involved, which are most easily learned from small specimens.

We will first undertake the work of skinning a small bird—a robin, thrush, or blackbird, whichever you happen to have. If in skinning, skin-making, and mounting you master the robin, for example, which is the highest type of a bird, you will be well prepared for the great majority of the other members of the feathered tribe.

Shoot your specimen with as fine shot as possible, and not too much even of that, in order to avoid shooting its mandibles, feet, legs, and feathers to pieces. As soon as it is dead, plug the throat, nostrils, and *all wounds that bleed*, with bits of cotton, to keep the blood and other liquids from oozing out upon the feathers, and putting you to more serious trouble. Carry the specimen home in any careful way you choose, so as to avoid rumpling or soiling the plumage. By all means let your first practice be upon clean birds.

FIG. 10.—Names of the External Parts of a Bird.* 1, Crown; 2, forehead; 3 nostrils (or cere); 4, upper mandible; 5, lower mandible; 6, throat; 7, neck; 8, spurious quills; 9, occiput; 10, ear; 11, nape; 12, breast; 13, middle coverts; 14, large coverts; 15, belly; 16, tibia; 17 tarsus; 18, inner toe; 19, middle toe; 20, outer toe; 21, thumb; 22, under-tail coverts; 23 tail; 24, primaries; 25, secondaries; 26, tertiaries.

A bird should lie an hour or two after being shot, in order

that the blood may coagulate. Warm specimens bleed very badly in skinning.

We are now in our workroom, with the gun standing quietly in its corner, and a robin lying on the table before us. Look at it. Study its form and structure, and remember what you see. Notice how smoothly the feathers lie—how nicely they fall over the angle of the wing at the shoulder—how completely the thigh is buried in the feathers of the breast and side, and also where the legs emerge from the body feathers. Notice how short the neck is, how the eye does *not* bulge out of the head, and note the fact that the breast and belly look full, round, and comfortable, instead of presenting that ghastly, drawn-up, eviscerated appearance so often seen in the amateur's mounted specimens. Note the color of the eye, the bill, the cere, tarsi, claws, and all other parts that will require painting when the specimen is mounted, if it ever should be. Now take the following

MEASUREMENTS.—It would be high treason for me to recommend any other system of bird measurement than that directed by Dr. Coues in his incomparable "Key to North American Birds," and it is hereby set forth:

1. *Length.*—Distance between the tip of the bill and the end of the longest feather of the tail.

2. *Extent of wings.*—This means the distance between the tips of the outstretched wings as the bird lies flat upon its

back.

3. *Length of wing.*—Distance from the angle formed at the (carpus) bend of the wing to the end of the largest primary. In birds with a convex wing, do not lay the tape-line over the curve, but under the wing, in a straight line.

4. *Length of the tail.*—Distance from the roots of the tail feathers to the end of the longest one. Feel for the "pope's nose;" in either a fresh or dried specimen there is more or less of a palpable lump into which the tail feathers stick. Guess as near as you can to the middle of this lump; place the end of the ruler opposite the point, and see where the tip of the longest tail feather comes.

5. *Length of bill.*—Dr. Coues takes "the chord of the culmen," which is determined thus: "Place one foot of the dividers on the culmen just where the feathers end; no matter whether the culmen runs up on the forehead, or the frontal feathers run out on the culmen, and no matter whether the culmen is straight or curved. With me the length of the bill is the shortest distance from the point indicated to the tip of the upper mandible."

6. *Length of tarsus.*—Distance between the joint of the tarsus with the leg above, and that with the first phalanx of the middle toe below. Measure it always with the dividers, and *in front* of the leg.

7. *Length of toes.*—Distance in a straight line along the

upper surface of a toe is from the point last indicated to the root of the claw on top. Length of toe is to be taken *without* the claw, unless otherwise specified.

8. *Length of the claws.*—Distance in a straight line from the point last indicated to the tip of the claw.

9. *Length of head.*—Set one foot of the dividers over the base of the culmen, and allow the other to slip just snugly down over the arch of the occiput.

For skinning a small bird, the only instrument imperatively necessary is a good-sized scalpel or a sharp penknife. You can use a pair of small scissors now and then, if you have them, to very good advantage, in severing legs and wings and clipping off tendons. Have ready a dish of corn meal to absorb any blood that is likely to soil the feathers. Now push a wad of cotton up the vent, and we are ready to remove the skin.

No, there is one thing more. The wings lie close to the body, and will be continually in our way unless we break them so that they will fall back and leave us a clear field. It is the humerus that must be snapped in two, as close to the body as possible. Those of small birds are easily broken with the thumb and finger, but in a large bird they must be treated to a sharp blow with a heavy stick, or a hammer.

Lay the bird upon its back, with its head toward your left hand; part the feathers in a straight line, and divide the skin from the *centre of the breast* straight down to the end of the breastbone, and on until the vent is reached. Cut through the skin only, for if you go too deep and cut through the wall of the abdomen you will have the intestines and various other troubles upon your hands.

Skin down each side of the bird until you come to the knee-joint, which lies close to the body, and well within the skin. Sever each leg completely at the knee, leaving the thigh attached to the body, turn the skin of the leg wrong side out over the fleshy part, quite down to the joint, and then cut away every particle of flesh from the bone of the leg.

Sever the tail from the body close to the ends of the tail feathers, without cutting through the skin. Now take the body between the thumb and forefinger of the left hand, holding it at the hips, and with the other hand separate the skin from the back. From this point we proceed to turn the skin wrong side out over the shoulders and head. When the wings are reached, cut them off where they are broken, and turn the skin down over the neck. Avoid cutting through the crop. If blood flows at any time, absorb it all with the corn meal or plaster Paris.

Almost before you know it you have skinned your bird down to the head, for it hangs head downward during the latter part of the operation, suspended on a small wire hook thrust through the pelvis, so that you can work with both hands.

It is a trifle more difficult to turn the skin over the head.

Push it up from the back of the head with the thumb-nail, working it patiently at all points, and stretching the skin gradually until it will pass over the widest part of the skull. Presently the crisis is past, the skin slips down without trouble, and we see by the way it is held at a certain point on each side of the head that we have come to the ears. Cut through the skin close up to the head, and a little farther on we reach the eyes.

FIG. 11.—First Steps in Skinning a Bird.

Now be careful. Cut very slowly at the eye, and close to the head, until you can see through the thin membrane and define the exact position of the eyeball. Now cut through the membrane, but do not cut the eyelid on any account. A little farther and we come to the base of the bill, where the skin and our skinning stops.

Cut through the back of the skull so as to sever the head completely from the neck, and lay bare the base of the brain. Remove the brain from the skull; cut the eyes out of their sockets; cut out the tongue and remove all flesh from the skull.

Skin each wing down to the first joint, or the elbow, and stop the "wrong-side-out" process there. The ends of the secondaries must not be separated from the bone of the forearm, or the ulna. It is possible to clean out the flesh from the forearm and also from the arm bone (humerus) without detaching the ends of the secondaries, as you will readily see. Cut away any flesh which has been left at the root of the tail, but do not cut the ends of the tail feathers.

The next thing is to poison the skin. Do this with a mixture of powdered arsenic and alum, in equal parts. Some of our most extensive collectors use no alum, simply pure arsenic in liberal quantity; but I consider that the use of alum also is always desirable, and under certain conditions it is extremely so. Some collectors use arsenical soap exclusively, even on small birds, and on large birds I, too, have used it quite extensively, supplemented by an immediate sprinkling of powdered alum, to do the curing of the skin. For genuine thoroughness in poisoning and preserving, I will back arsenical soap and alum against all other substances the world can produce; but in treating *small birds that are to be made up as dry skins*, I prefer and recommend powdered arsenic and alum, as stated above.

Whatever poison you decide to use, apply it thoroughly to every part of the skin, the skull, wings, legs, and tail. Now put a ball of cotton in each eye-socket to fill up the cavity, and you are ready to reverse the skin and bring it right side out once more. It is usually some trouble to get the skin back over the skull, and that I accomplish in this wise:

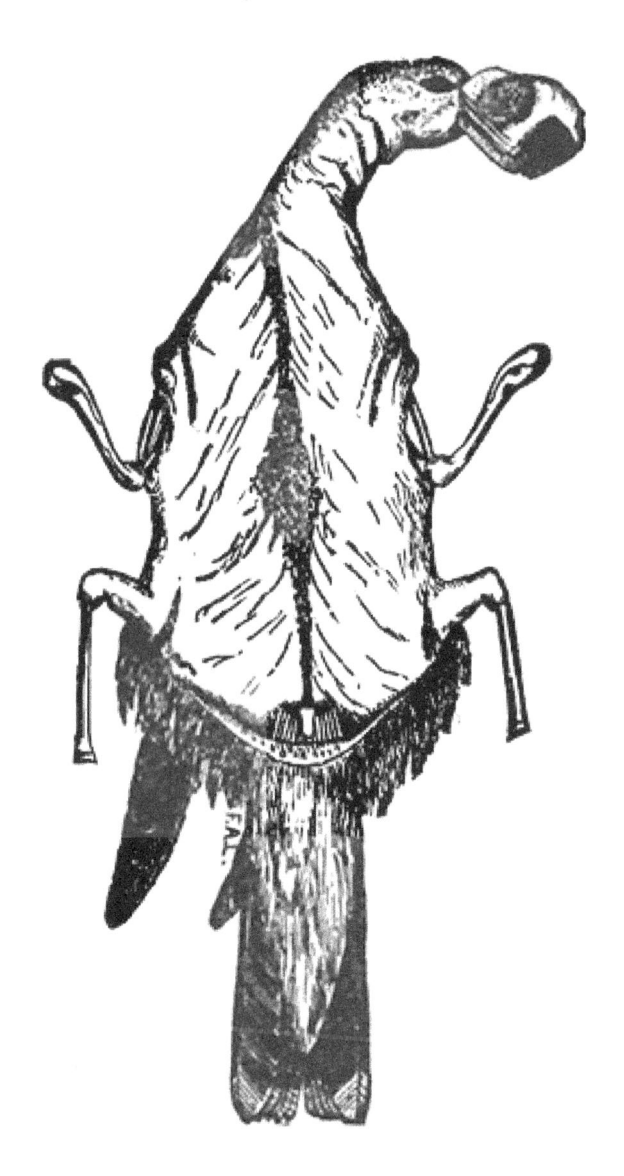

FIG. 12.—The Skin Wrong Side Out, and Ready to be Poisoned.

Let the skin rest on the edge of the table, place both of your thumbs on the back of the skull, and with all your fingers and finger-nails, reach forward and begin to crowd the skin of the head back where it belongs. At the same time, you must push on the skull with your thumbs, as if trying to push it into the neck, and in a very short time, by a combination of coaxing and crowding, the skin made passes the critical point on the skull, and, presto! the whole skin is right side out once more. Now take it by the bill and give it a gentle shaking to stir up the feathers so that they will fall back naturally. Pluck outward the cotton in the orbit into the opening of the eye, to imitate the round fulness of the eyeball.

The wing bones of very small birds need not be wrapped with cotton, but the leg bones should be, always. Now take a bunch of cotton batting of the right size, and roll it between the palms until it attains the proper size to fill the neck, and is a trifle longer than the entire body and neck. Fold over one end of this, take it between the points of your forceps, insert it through the neck, and into the cavity of the skull. Tuck up the other end at the tail, and give the cotton body its right length. Then in the middle of the skin, pull the cotton roll apart sidewise, spread it out and lay on it a ball of cotton to form the body.

Next, take hold of the broken humerus with the forceps, and pull it inward until the joint of the wing appears, and the two humeri lie parallel and close to each other. This draws the wings into place.

Be sure to put enough cotton in the body of a skin; for a little plumpness and rotundity is desirable in a small skin. Avoid making cylindrical bird skins; avoid the East Indian native habit of crowding the breast of a bird clear up into its neck, and also avoid stretching a skin.

We have now to finish the head by inserting a little bunch of cotton in the throat, until that part is properly filled, and plucking out or cutting off the surplus. The mandibles must be held together by a thread or a pin until they have dried in position. Next adjust the wings, legs, and tail. The tail should be slightly spread, and there are two ways of doing this. One is to reverse the natural overlapping of the tail feathers, which is the quickest way, and quite satisfactory. The other is to lay the skin on a board, put a pin through each corner of the "pope's nose," spread the tail, and thrust the pins into the board until the skin is dry. Finally, tie on your label, which should be as small as possible to contain the necessary data—locality, date, sex, number, collector's name, measurements, and remarks. Some collectors label only with numbers, corresponding with recorded data in a note-book; but it is a bad plan. Note-books often get lost, and then such specimens lose half their value.

FIG. 13.—The Bird Skin in Position.

WRAPPING UP A SKIN.—There are various ways of "laying out" bird skins. The best is to wrap each skin in a very thin sheet of cotton batting or wadding, which draws with the softness of down, and yet, when pinched or twisted at the ends, it holds every feather in place. The bird skins prepared by Mr. William Palmer, one of the National Museum taxidermists, are fine examples of how skins should be made. Mr. Palmer's method of shaping and wrapping up a small skin is as follows, and the accompanying figures are from specimens prepared by him: Take the skin up between the left thumb and forefinger, at the shoulders, and pinch it together, while with the small forceps you adjust the scapulars over the point of the wings. Cross the feet, lay the skin breast downward on a thin sheet of cotton batting of the proper dimensions, and arrange the feathers of the back, the wings, etc. (Fig. 13). Then lift the outer edge of the sheet of cotton, bring it forward over the skin toward the operator, so that it will cover the back (Fig. 14). Next, lift the inner edge of the cotton sheet, draw it with gentle pressure to make the skin of the right size, and lap it well over the other. The two edges of the cotton sheet will stick together very well by simply overlapping them.

The head can be adjusted by pulling on the cotton at that end, and pinching the end together beyond the head. The bill must be set at the proper angle, and held by catching the point in the cotton. Do not let the bill point straight out, for it will stretch the skin of the throat too much; neither should it point up at a right angle to the body, for the tip will be catching in everything that comes near it. The best way with most short-billed birds is to let the bill point at an angle of about forty-five degrees to the axis of the body. Beaks that are very long require special arrangement, as shown in Figs. 17 and 18.

FIG. 14.—The Skin Half Wrapped.

Now lift the wrapped-up skin, lay it with the tail toward you, breast uppermost, and with both hands tear the cotton open in a straight line up to the base of the tail (Fig. 15). You can now spread the tail by overlapping the feathers, or leave it closed if you prefer. See that your label is on, adjust the toes and legs carefully, then fold over the edges of the cotton and overlap them, and the skin is done (Fig. 16). Always spread the toes of all swimming-birds.

Another plan is to dispose of each skin in a little cylinder of paper, made to fit, of course. This is the best plan when you are far from the conveniences of home, and in a hurry. The effect of this, however, is to produce a cylindrical skin, which is not a prize shape. Still another way is to make a small cornucopia of stiff paper, and slip the skin into it, head first, after which the large end is closed by bending in the edges. The old-fashioned, corrugated drying-board is an excellent resource when you are in a great hurry with a number of specimens.

FIG. 15.—Spreading the Tail.

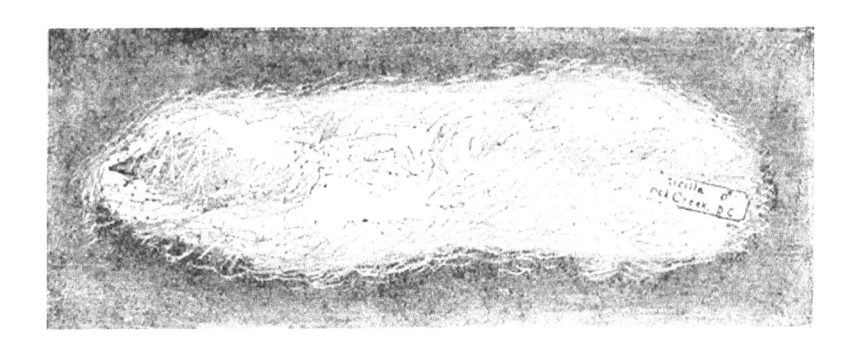

FIG. 16.—The Skin fully Wrapped.

The illustration on p. 56 (Fig. 17), from one of Mr. Palmer's specimens, shows the shape a small skin should have to be considered perfect.

Freshly made bird skins should never be subjected to crowding or pressure, nor should old skins either, for that matter. If you go far afield, and expect to collect hundreds of skins, you should go provided with a light and strong chest, either made to open at one side and contain a series of shallow drawers to receive skins, or else, which is the next best thing, and very easily made, a box containing a series of shallow tills of varying depth, standing one upon another from bottom to top. Each drawer or till should be made just deep enough to hold skins of a certain size, but no more, or else in travelling the skins will tumble about. Remember it is useless to try to make large collections of good skins in the field unless you can take care of your finished specimens. This is for specimens freshly prepared and *not yet dry*. After skins become thoroughly dry, they can be packed "in bulk," in a chest or trunk, by putting the largest at the bottom, and filling the cavities with the small skins which cannot stand so much pressure. Bird skins should always be packed in cotton when they are to be shipped, giving to each a soft, comfortable resting-place, and the box must be filled full, so that there will be no tossing about.

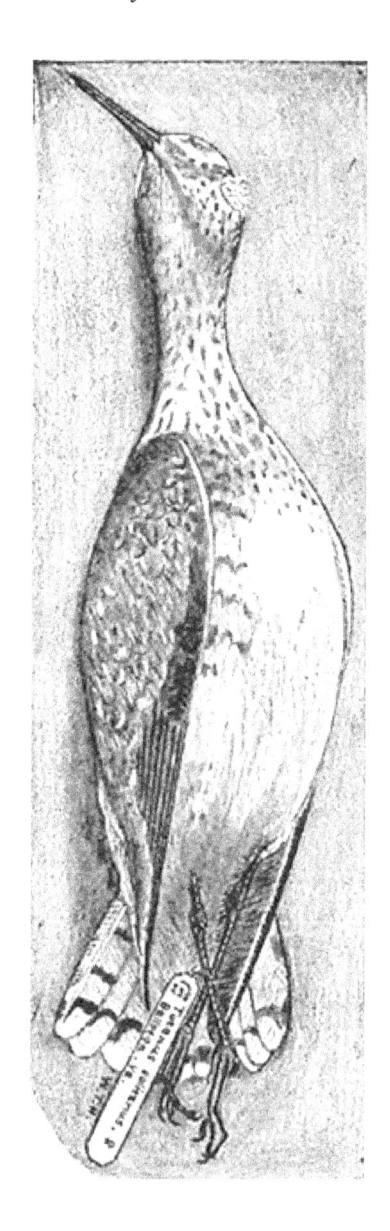

FIG. 17.—A Perfect Bird Skin.

DETERMINATION OF SEX IN BIRDS.—To a collector who is working under difficulties this often seems like the very "last straw upon a camel's back;" but it must be attended to in every case wherein the sex of the bird is not clearly and unmistakably indicated by the plumage. If you can, get an experienced ornithologist to show you how to determine the sex in difficult subjects (*e.g.*, young birds, or birds midway between two breeding seasons). But there are ways in which we can help ourselves. If you begin with birds during or near the breeding season, you will have plain sailing long enough to become familiar with the subject.

In birds the organs of generation lie close up to the lumbar vertebræ, near the kidneys, in the region called "the small of the back." The best way to reach this region for examination is to make a cut clear across the wall of the abdomen, break the back over at the last pair of ribs, and the intestines will at once fall down, exposing the lumbar region. You will then see the kidneys—two large, dark-brown masses situated in the concavity of the sacrum—and on their surface, at the upper end, lie the reproductive organs. The testicles of the male are two dull, whitish, ellipsoidal, or nearly round bodies, of the same size, lying close together. The sign for this sex is the astronomical sign for the planet Mars (♂).

The ovary of the female is, except during the breeding season, the most difficult to distinguish. Look first for a little bunch of minute round globules, of varying sizes and grayish-white color. In the breeding season the eggs are easily found. Failing in that, you must look for the ovary itself, which, when found, will be recognized as a little, irregular, flattish bunch of a light gray color. If you search with a magnifying-glass, you may be able to detect it by its peculiar granulated appearance.

The sign for the female is the sign for the planet Venus (♀).

Skinning Birds

Birds should never be skinned while they are warm, for the blood will flow out and is apt to soil the plumage. While these stains can be removed, yet it is a difficult matter and it is best not to get the blood on the feathers when it can be avoided.

Kill specimens several hours before you expect to work on them, or better still, allow them to lie over night. In cool weather a bird can be mounted after it has been dead for several days. In hot climates, however, they should be skinned as soon as they become stiff and the blood has become thick or coagulated. When a bird has been dead the required time, you may prepare for actual skinning. Get all the tools and material ready before you start. You should have a work table, which should be covered with paper, having an extra supply on hand so that the paper can be changed when it becomes soiled during the skinning process.

FIG. 10.—Names of the External Parts of a Bird.* 1, Crown; 2, forehead; 3 nostrils (or cere); 4, upper mandible; 5, lower mandible; 6, throat; 7, neck; 8, spurious quills; 9, occiput; 10, ear; 11, nape; 12, breast; 13, middle coverts; 14, large coverts; 15, belly; 16, tibia; 17 tarsus; 18, inner toe; 19, middle toe; 20, outer toe; 21, thumb; 22, under-tail coverts; 23, tail; 24, primaries; 25, secondaries; 26, tertiaries.

(From Horniday)

The Operation

Place the bird on the table with the back down and the head at your left hand. Tie a thread firmly around the beak and fill the mouth, nostrils and the vent and all shot holes that bleed with fresh cotton to prevent the blood from flowing out and staining the feathers. Now you may separate the feathers on the middle of the breast from the point of the breast bone to the vent. You will discover a bare space throughout this length on almost all birds. It is a great boon to the Taxidermist.

Spread the feathers carefully to the right and left with the fingers, brush or sponge and continue to stroke them until they remain in this position.

Now take a sharp knife or scalpel and make an incision in the skin from the point of the breast bone entirely to the vent opening **(see figure 1),** being careful not to crush the flesh on the breast, as the blood and fluids will flow out and soil the plumage. Skin right and left from this incision, pushing the skin from the flesh. With the scissors or knife, cut all tissues that refuse to separate easily.

Fig. 1

Continue in this manner until you reach the junctures of the legs with the body **(figure 2)**. Now is the time that the corn meal is used. As soon as the flesh is exposed cover all parts with the meal in order to absorb the blood and moisture. Use it frequently as you proceed.

If the blood flows from any place, immediately apply cotton until the bleeding has ceased, and then cover the part heavily with dry plaster of Paris. Keep the feathers along the incision dry and brushed away from the opening. If the breast of the bird be white, we advise the student to place cloths over the edges of the skin and sew them fast with needle and thread until the skinning is done. This is an admirable thing to do when skinning all birds.

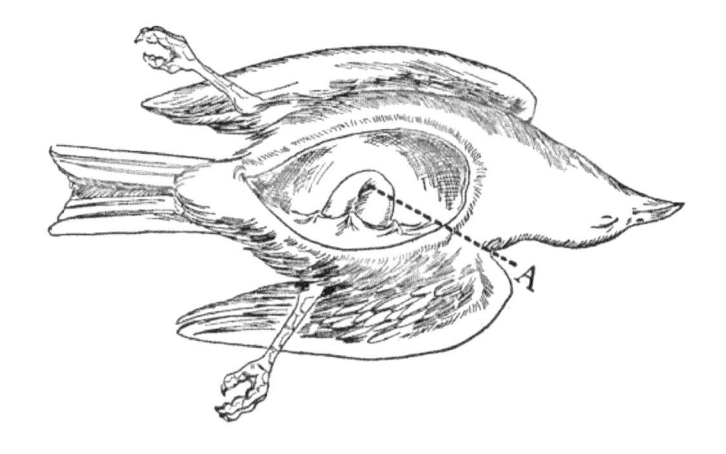

Fig. 2

Now grasp the leg and bend the knee joint, pushing it forward, and at the same time forcing the skin over the joint until it is exposed. Disconnect this joint at "A," **figure 2,** leaving the thigh on the body. Perform the same operation on the other leg. You can now, with your fingers, separate the skin from the body across the back in front of the tail.

With the knife or scissors cut through the base of the tail, leaving the tail feathers well imbedded, being careful not to cut the roots of these feathers, as they would fall out and the skin be ruined. Cut should be made on line "B," **figure 3**. The tail may be severed before the student attempts to skin across the back. When this is done great care should be exercised that the skin is not cut. Take your time. Work carefully. A little haste often spoils the specimen at this point.

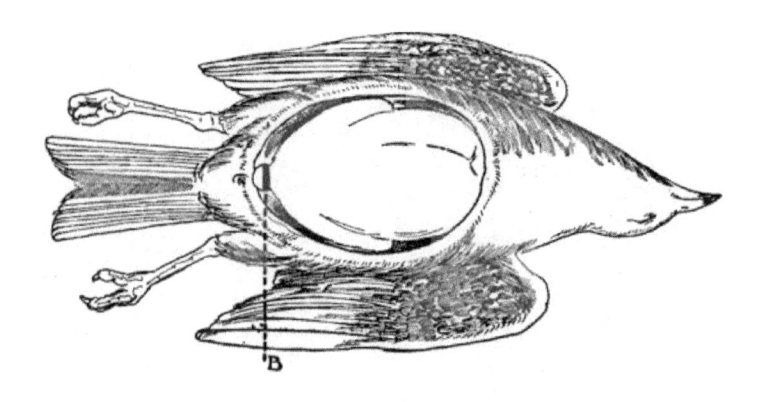

Fig. 3

After severing the tail, the rear part of the body is free from skin. It will now assist you to have a hook suspended from the ceiling at the proper height, and suspend the bird on the same, attaching it to the rump of the body **(figures 4 and 5)**. This is almost necessary with large specimens.

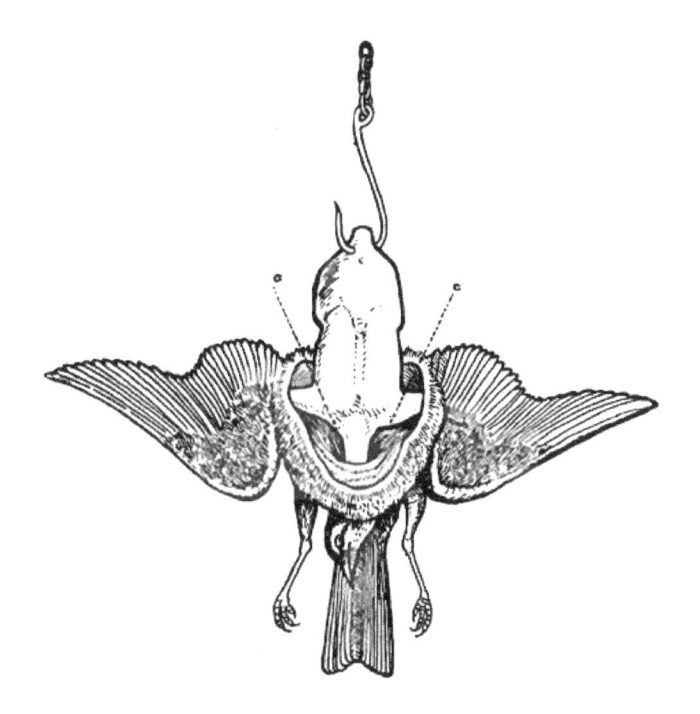

Fig. 4

Taxidermy - Vol. 2 Small Birds

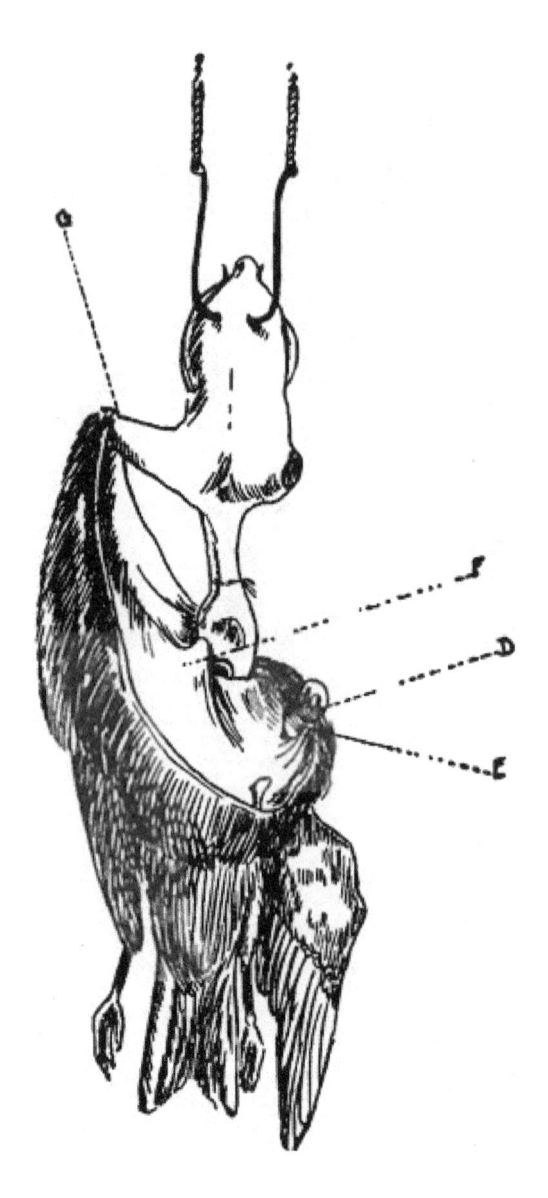

Fig. 5

You may now easily skin the body forward until the wings are reached. Detach them at the body point at "C," **figure 4,** and continue the skinning to the head, by inverting the skin over the head, as a person might remove a glove. Care must be used that the skin is not stretched.

Skinning the Head

When the head is reached, push the skin gently over the base of the skull, using the scalpel for cutting the tissue, when necessary. The ears are now reached. Cut the skin **close to the skull ("F," figure 5),** and continue to the eyes. A thin membrane will be found, which must be cut, using much care that the eyelids or balls are not injured.

After passing the eyes continue the skinning to the very base of the beak. Do not detach the skin from the head, but leave it fastened to the beak as shown in **figure 7**. After you have completed the skinning in this way cut off the head from the neck at the line "H" in **figure 6**. You should also cut off the back part of the skull, leaving the brain exposed as shown at "K" in **figure 7**.

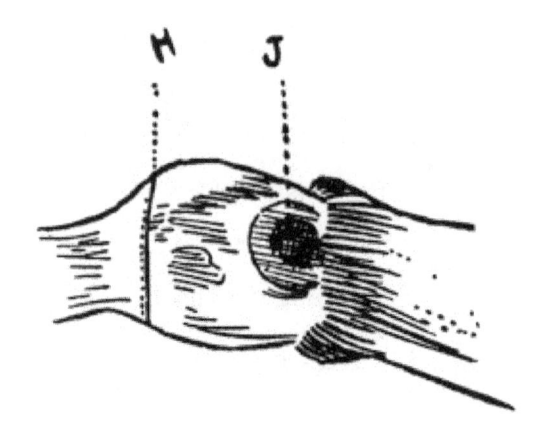

Fig. 6

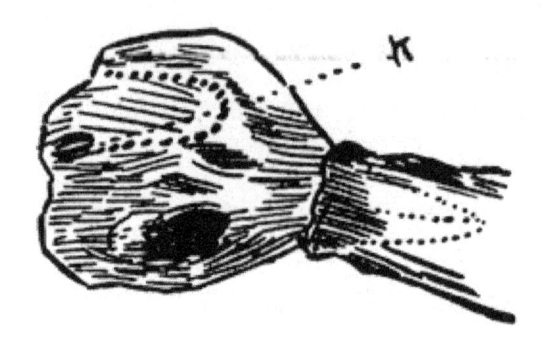

Fig. 7

You will note that the back and underside of the skull is removed, but do not cut away the top of the skull. Cut as shown by the dotted line in **figure 7**. Now dig out the brain with a brain spoon, being careful to get it all removed. Lift out the eyes **("J," figure 6),** using either a knife, scalpel or small block. Do not pierce the eye balls, as the fluid is apt to flow out and soil the feathers. Throw the eye balls away, as they are to be replaced later with artificial glass eyes.

Now cut and scrape away all flesh from the skull and remove the tongue, and on larger birds cut out the cartilage that forms the lining in the roof of the mouth. Do not detach the joint of the mandibles (or beak). It is very important that you get **all of the flesh removed** from all parts of the skull, for it will otherwise decay and cause the specimen to spoil. With the use of a scalpel, knife and scissors trim away all the fat that is clinging to the inside of the head and neck skin. Do all of this work rapidly, for it is necessary to turn the skin back over the skull before it becomes dry.

You will now cover the entire skull, inside and out, with a free application of the preserving powder. Get it into the "corners." The skin of the head and neck must also receive a liberal supply. Rub it well into the skin with several applications.

Fill each eye cavity with a ball of tow or hemp, or potter's clay. In small specimens the latter is to be preferred, and we often use it in the largest specimens, as it aids much in setting the artificial eyes. If tow is used be sure and wind it tight into a firm ball, of such size that it fills the cavity level full.

You are now ready to replace the skin over the head, which can be easily done after a few trials. Go slowly, pushing first at the top of the head and then underneath, as required. **Figure 8** gives a clear illustration of how this should be done.

Remember that this work must be done **as soon as possible,** as the skin quickly dries after the preserving powder has been applied, and is then difficult to perform. If, however, the skin should become a little dry, simply dampen the skull with a wet sponge and the task will be much facilitated. The feathers have doubtless become much disarranged by this turning inside-out process, and you must now restore them to their original positions.

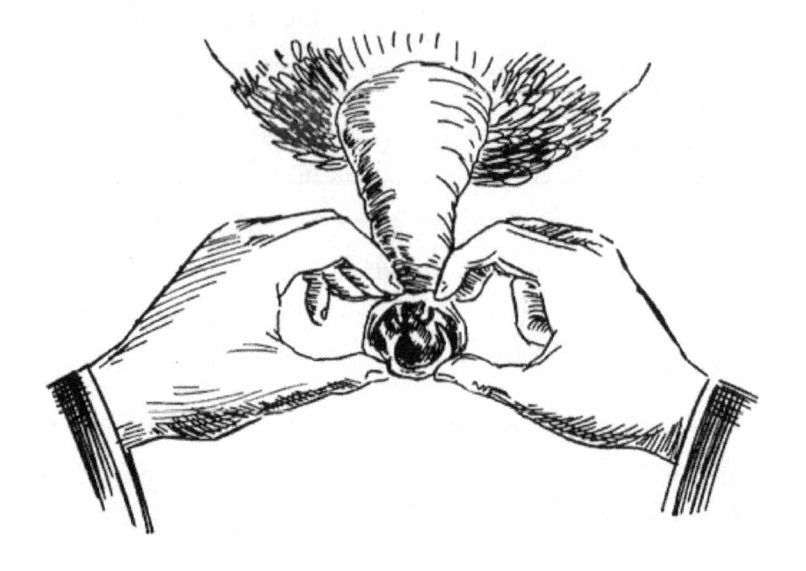

Fig. 8

First take the specimen by the bill and shake it briskly. After this insert a darning needle through the eye opening and rub the inside of the neck and head with considerable force, when you will find the feathers assume their natural positions readily. **(Figure 9.)** Do not be afraid to rub and stroke the feathers with hands and a brush, even quite hard, for they are often obstinate.

Fig. 9

In mounting small specimens up to the size of a crow, it is not necessary to replace the flesh and muscles that you have cut off from the skull, but on larger birds such as ducks, owls, hawks, eagles, etc., these muscles must be restored or the specimens will not have the right shape and appearance. When mounting these larger birds you should replace the muscles with potter's clay while the skin is removed from the skull. Mix the potter's clay with water until it is smooth and soft and place it on the skull to take the place of the removed muscles. You can easily do this, as the clay will be wet and soft and the skin will slip back over it readily.

Skinning the Legs

We will now give our attention to the legs, which we have detached from the natural body and which have not yet been skinned. Invert the skin over the leg bone as far down as the heel joint; the heel in a bird being the first joint above the foot; see **figure 10**. In some birds, such as owls, where the feathers grow entirely to the feet, the legs should be skinned the full length, or as far down as the feathers grow.

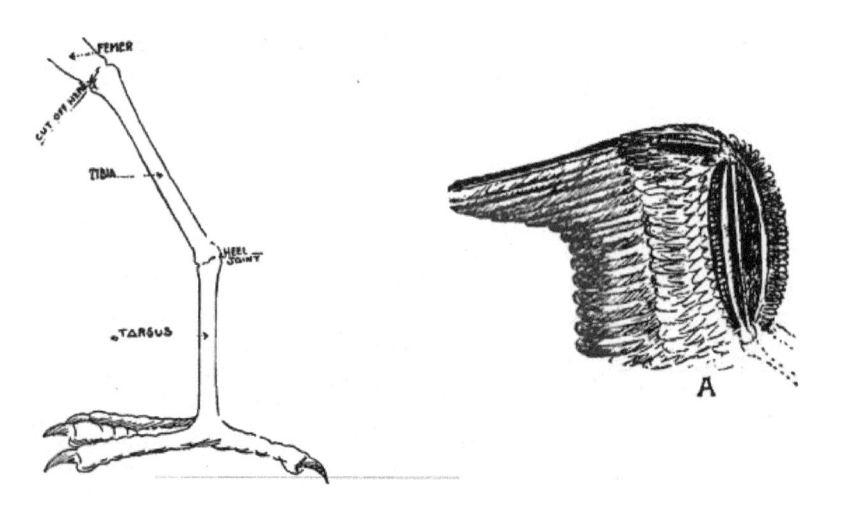

Fig. 10

Remove all the muscles and flesh from the leg bones, using a scalpel, bone scraper and scissors. Be sure and get every particle of flesh off the bone. After the flesh is removed the skin can be drawn back over the bone. In larger specimens it is necessary to cut open the bottom of the feet and remove the tendons from the legs. This process is discussed later in this lesson.

Skinning the Wings

First lay the wing flat on the table so you have a solid base to work on, then open the wing on the under side by making a cut the whole length of the large bones in each part and skin the wings in the same manner that you skinned the legs, by inverting the skin over the bone until you reach the first joint. Do not attempt to invert the skin beyond the first bone, called the "humerus." In **figure 5,** point "G" shows how far to invert the skin. "D" represents the one wing bone properly skinned. Study these illustrations carefully. Cut and scrape all the fat from the humerus bone and then bring the skin back to its original position.

Figure A shows clearly the two cuts to be made. Hold up the outer row of feathers and make the incision. Scrape and cut away all the fat and flesh possible, but do not detach the large feathers where they are anchored. After this is done, sprinkle preserving powder liberally along the wing bones. It is not necessary to sew up these incisions in the wings, as the feathers will fall back and conceal the cuts.

Another method which you will do well to try out. Place the wing on the table and lift the entire third row of feathers by inserting a long knife blade between the second and third row of feathers, counting from the tips of the long secondary feathers. Holding the feathers back with the left hand, make a cut along the bone of the wing, using a sharp scalpel. Skin back the flap until both bones are exposed. Remove all flesh and muscles. Apply arsenical paste thoroughly. Touch the under feathers lightly with a little flour paste, brush the feathers smooth and the job is done.

After skinning both of the wings as instructed above, cut off the large joints. Do not cut away all of the bone, but just the enlarged parts, as shown by the line "E" in **figure 5**. These joints are only in the way when you come to mounting the skin.

You may find it a little difficult to skin out the wings in this way at first, but after you have performed the work a number of times, it will be very easy and simple.

Next give your attention to the cartilage of the tail. Cut away most of the fat and flesh, but do not remove enough to loosen the tail feathers. If you do, you will then have serious trouble. Leave sufficient cartilage so that the feathers are anchored firmly. You should apply the preserving powder very liberally about the base of the tail, as there is more flesh left there than on any other part of the body. If enough preservation is used, you are not going to have any difficulty with the specimens spoiling.

Now go over the whole interior of the skin with a scalpel, scissors, and fat scraper, removing all of the clinging fat and flesh. In many specimens there is a great deal of fat, but on common birds it is not a very big job to get the inside of the skin thoroughly cleaned.

After you have the inside of the skin free from fat and flesh, **give the whole interior a liberal application of the preserving powder**. Rub it in well, using a brush, cloth or wooden paddle. Be sure that all parts are reached. You now have the skinning operations completed.

The feathers must be nicely picked out and the skin arranged in a neat, smooth position. Extend the legs backward and insert a small roll of cotton into the neck, and another roll into the body, so that the sides of the skin will not lie together. After each feather is in its place, wrap the skin in soft paper or sheet cotton and lay it away some place, out of reach of children. It is now **poisoned,** and ready to be mounted. Before putting the skin away, however, you should look it over and see if there are any fresh blood spots, and if so, wash them away with a cloth and warm water. You will have no difficulty in removing them if they are fresh, but if they become dry it takes considerable work. If your first attempt has resulted in a skin fairly free from cuts you can congratulate yourself on the job.

While at first thought it seems a difficult matter to skin a bird and have the skin free from cuts and tears, yet after a few trials you will find that you can do it easily, and that the work requires just a short time. Do not be discouraged if you have the skin torn to pieces on your first effort. I can assure you after you have removed skins from a half dozen or more birds you will be able to take them off perfectly.

Remember that Practice—Practice—Practice is what is required in order to master this art in its details and to become thoroughly competent.

After you have the work completed and the skin laid away you may turn your attention to the original body from which you have removed the skin. Measure its exact length and also diameter in two or three places, using a caliper and tape measure for this purpose. You should also measure the distance around the body at the breast and in the middle and record these measurements for use when you commence to mount the skin. After you have worked on birds for some time you will not need to take these measurements, as you will know from experience just what sizes the bodies should be for the various birds.

Other Points to Be Carefully Observed Birds with Large Heads

With some specimens such as ducks, flickers, cranes, etc., the skull is so large that the neck skin cannot be easily inverted over it. When skinning these specimens it is necessary to make an additional incision on the throat or the back of the head. We prefer the latter, although many successful Taxidermists use the throat-cut. The incision should be made in the middle of the back of the head, about an inch long in small birds, while in larger birds it must of course be longer.

In skinning the head you should invert the skull through this opening instead of trying to force it through the full length of the neck. **Figure 11** shows how the cut should be made in a duck's head. It also shows how you can set the bill of the duck in a hole in the table to hold it in position while you are performing the work. After you have skinned out the head, remove the fat and apply the preservative.

Fig. 11

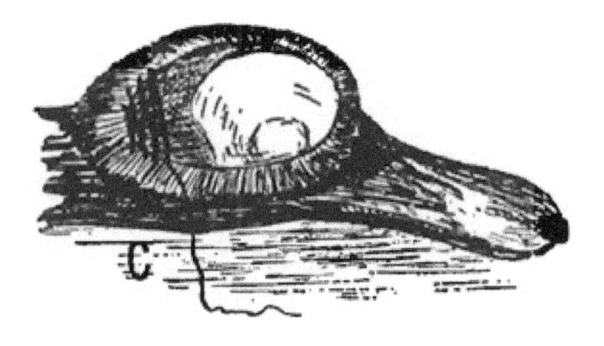

Fig. 12

You should restore the skull to its original position and sew up the opening immediately. This point is illustrated in **figure 12**. A number of birds such as wood ducks, hooded mergansers, etc., which have topknots, should have the incision made lower down on the back of the head, as you should not attempt to cut through the feathers of the head forming the top-knot.

Birds with White Breasts

In skinning birds with white breasts or those having the entire plumage white, you must handle them with much care. If you get the feathers bloody, it is a difficult matter to restore them to their original whiteness. When skinning such specimens you can make the incision under the wing instead of down the breast if you prefer, yet we think that you will have better results by sticking to the breast cut. After making the incision in the regular way you can separate the skin a short distance on each side of the incision and then sew cloths over the edges to protect the feathers. It is also a good plan to do this when skinning birds that are very fat. It is always easier to prevent the plumage from becoming soiled than to clean it after it becomes greasy or bloody.

Removing Tendons

You should remove the tendons from the feet and legs of all large birds. In birds the size of a quail or pigeon, it is not necessary to open the bottom of the feet nor to remove the tendons between the foot and knee joint, but on all large birds this is absolutely necessary. In order to perform the work properly you should split open the bottom of the foot and bottom of each toe and cut out the tendons from the toes, and then take a pair of pliers and pull out the tendon from the leg. We illustrate how this is done in **figure 13**. It is, of course, necessary to have the lower end of the tendon cut loose and free so that you can get hold of it with a pair of pliers. Some Taxidermists use a hook wire instead of pliers in pulling out the tendons, but the pliers are better if you can grasp the tendons with them.

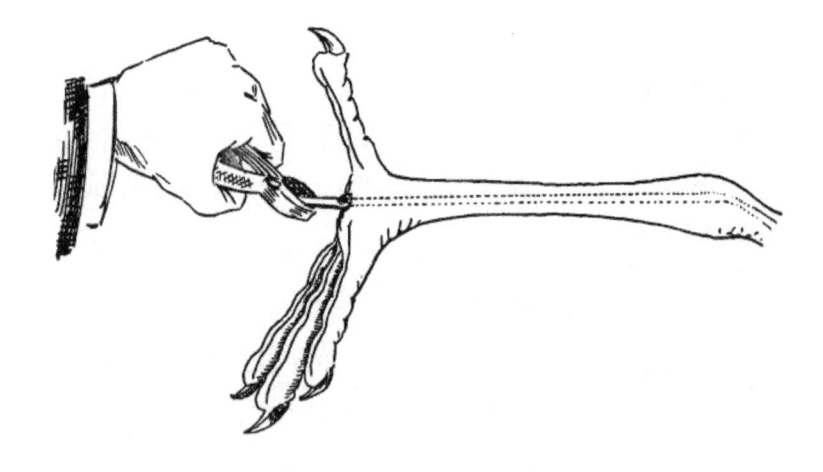

Fig. 13

Removing Fat from Skins

All sea birds are very fat. When skinning them use meal and plaster freely, and protect the feathers in all ways possible, as the fat is hard to remove. If, however, the feathers along the incision become soiled with the fat, they may be cleaned in a satisfactory manner by the use of gasoline, drying the same with applications of plaster. The interior of the skins of these birds is covered with fat which must be thoroughly removed. This is done by applying corn meal freely, and scraping it away with a fat scraper. An old table knife with the edge filed into small notches answers very nicely. In any event be sure to clean the skin well, with many applications of the meal, as otherwise the specimen is hard to preserve, and after several months the fat may work its way through the plumage and discolor it, at the same time inviting ravages from insects.

The Proper Bones to Use

We wish to make it entirely clear to you what bones should be retained when you are mounting birds. The following bones and no others are ever used: The **skull, all** of the **wing bones,** and all of the leg bones, **except the thigh bone,** or femur. Examine **figure 10**. You should use the tibia and tarsus, but **not** the femur. When you are skinning a bird, note that the heel is at the first joint above the foot and not at the foot itself. Usually the skinning extends over the femur only, except in birds where the feathers grow entirely to the foot. You should then invert the skin as far as the feathers grow. Sometimes the bones of the legs and wings are broken by a shot. In such cases they should be repaired by inserting a wire of the proper size, or a little hardwood stick, into the two ends of the broken bone and winding same firmly with copper wire or small stout twine.

Colors

As soon as the specimen has been secured, note carefully the exact colors of the feet, bill and other exposed parts, as they are apt to fade soon after death and must be restored by the use of paints, as shown in a later lesson. If you are familiar with the use of paints it is a good plan to make the exact colors of these parts on paper, to be used later when you are restoring the colors of your bird. You should also note carefully the exact color of the eyes so that you can select the proper artificial glass ones when you come to set them in the specimens.

There are many little details of this kind that you will become familiar with by actual practice.

Here Are a Few More Points That You Should Carefully Observe

1. It is sometimes necessary to mount birds when they are badly spoiled. If the feathers are slipping seriously you cannot do anything with the specimens, but if they are just a trifle loose apply the preservative and the feathers may soon set and become tight again. If the feathers above the head are a little loose, I would recommend that you split the back of the head whether the skull is large or not, as it does not bring so much strain on the feathers when inverting the skin over the skull. It is also a good plan to dust the head feathers with dry soapstone or talcum powder, as it assists very much when forcing the skull back through the neck skin. You should never put anything of this kind on the feathers unless they are perfectly dry.

2. In skinning owls you are apt to cut great gashes in the ears, unless you are very careful. You should detach the ears of owls deeply in the skull. A little experience will teach you

just what we mean, and after you have handled a few you will have no difficulty. Around the eyeball in owls there is a bony structure called the eye cup. This must be left in place to assist in giving expression to the face. After removing the eyeballs you clean the eye cups and eye cavity thoroughly. Or you may take them out and clean them. If you do this you must put them back in place, as they serve a special purpose. In skinning hawks you will find that there are two extra small bones on the skull, just above the eyes. These should be left attached to the skull and not thrown away, as they are needed in giving the face the correct expression.

3. One of the most difficult specimens to mount satisfactorily is the domestic rooster with large comb. The most successful way of handling this specimen is to make a wax cast of the comb and attach it onto the head in place of the natural one. This is not to be undertaken in ordinary work, as it requires much skill and continued practice. If you desire to mount a specimen of this kind, I would recommend that you poison the comb thoroughly by applying corrosive sublimate dissolved in alcohol. After this is done, hold the comb and wattles in position by packing around them wet potter's clay and allowing them to become dry. You can then break the clay away and the comb will retain its position and shape. You will, of course, have to paint it with oil paints to restore the natural colors.

Conclusion

You have now learned how to skin birds properly for mounting. Perform this lesson several times before you attempt number two. as you will need a good sound skin for your first attempt at mounting. This lesson necessarily is of less interest than any other in the course, as it deals simply with skinning. Number two is one of the most interesting. In it you will learn how to mount the specimen. You see the results of your labor and enjoy the process of restoring the now shapeless skin to a beautiful bird, as natural as the living one. In it you get the real art of Taxidermy, and commence to appreciate what this knowledge will mean to you. In conclusion, we feel that we must again warn you against impatience and haste. This lesson is but one of the steps that will be taken in your progress, and as stated above, may be devoid of particular interest to the beginner, yet it is very important, as the results of your mounting depend largely on how well the specimen is skinned. We believe that you will await your second lesson with pleasant anticipation, as it contains much of interest, and completes the first steps of mounting birds. You will need a few additional tools, and we advise you to have in readiness a quantity of wire, assorted in sizes from 10 to 16, a file, pliers, a quantity of tow, excelsior, cotton, and twine string. You will also need a small assortment of artificial glass eyes. These can be secured from any dealer in supplies at a few cents per pair. If the student desires, he can send his order direct to us, though we wish him to feel free to buy where he pleases. Our eyes are of good quality, and are sold cheaper than the usual price. We recommend a small order at first, as you can decide better after a few weeks just what you will need.

Remember that nothing will take the place of actual practice, and that by following our lessons carefully, and making good use of the privilege of asking questions and referring all obscure points to us for additional explanation, you will succeed beyond your most ardent expectations.

Supply Catalog

At the same time this lesson book was mailed to you, we also sent you, under separate cover, our latest catalog of Taxidermy Supplies, and Glass Eyes. We carry the most complete stock of Taxidermy Supplies in the United States. If you do not receive the catalog within a week, kindly write us and we will send you another one. When you get ready to purchase tools or materials, we will guarantee you prompt, satisfactory service.

J. W. ELWOOD, Pres.
THE NORTHWESTERN SCHOOL OF TAXIDERMY,
Omaha, Nebraska

*From Steele's Popular Zoology, by permission of the American Book Company.

MOUNTING SMALL BIRDS

WE will suppose that the skin of a small bird—a robin, blackbird, or thrush—now lies on the table before us all ready for mounting. Perhaps it is a dry skin which has been thoroughly relaxed, scraped, and worked into pliant shape; but, for the sake of the beginner, we will assume that it is a fresh skin which has just been taken off, poisoned, and turned right side out again, in accordance with the directions for skinning small birds which have been given in Chapter VI. The body of the bird lies before you, and instead of making up the subject as a dry skin, we will mount it.

In mounting small birds the following tools are absolutely necessary to the production of good results: A pair of flat-nosed pliers six inches long, for bending and clinching wires, price sixty cents; a pair of six-inch cutting pliers, for cutting wire, eighty-five cents; a pair of bird-stuffer's forceps, four to six inch, price twenty to seventy-five cents; a nine-inch flat file, twenty-two cents. Make for yourself a stuffing-rod, by taking a piece of *stiff* brass or iron wire, a little larger and longer than a knitting-needle, hammering one end flat, with a slight upward curve, and inserting the other in an awl-handle.

Of materials you will need some excelsior; some clean, fine

tow; a little putty or potter's clay; a spool of cotton thread, No. 40, and some suitable glass eyes. With our tools and materials ready at hand, and the skin of our bird lying before us right side out, we are ready to begin a new operation,—mounting.

For a bird the size of a robin or cat-bird, cut two pieces of No. 18 soft or "annealed" iron wire (hard wire heated red hot and allowed to cool slowly), each three times the length of the bird's legs, from foot to end of long leg-bone, or tarsus. File one end of each wire to a slender and very sharp point, and rub a little oil or grease on each so that it will easily slip when inside the leg.

Now take one of the bird's legs between the thumb and finger of the left hand, holding it at the foot with the back part uppermost, and with the other hand enter the point of one of the sharpened wires at the centre of foot, push the wire up the *back* of the leg and over the heel until the point reaches to where the leg has been skinned. Be sure that you do not run the wire up the *side* of the leg, either at foot or knee, for if you do it will show badly when the bird is dry. Also be careful not to run the sharpened wire out through the skin just above the heel. To avoid this, grasp the leg at the heel between the thumb and middle finger of left hand, and by strong upward pressure of the first finger under the end of the leg-bone, and of the fourth finger under the foot, both joints of the leg can be held exactly in line until the wire passes the heel safely and enters the open skin above (Fig. 48). Then we turn back the skin of the leg till we see the point of the wire, after which we push the wire on up until the point passes the end of the leg bone. We now cut off the thick upper end of this bone, (the tibia), and wrap a little fine tow smoothly around the bone and the wire, to replace the flesh cut away. The other leg must, of course, be similarly treated. We are now ready to make the body.

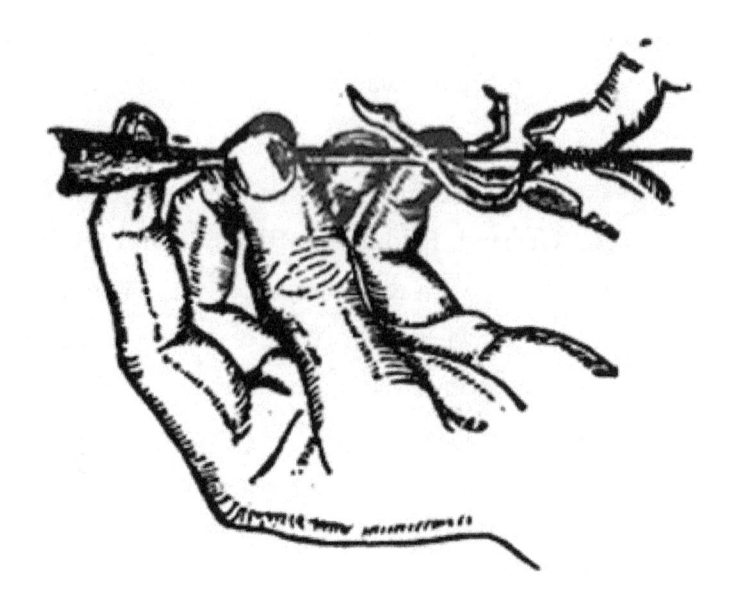

FIG. 48.—Wiring a Bird's Leg.

We have kept the body of our specimen for reference, and now we measure the length of both body and neck, cut another wire not quite twice their length and file it sharp at both ends. This will be the neck-wire. Now take a handful of excelsior (tow or oakum will also serve), compress it into an egg-shaped ball—smaller and more pointed at one end than the other, and wrap a very little fine tow loosely around it, to make it smooth on the outside when finished. Now wind stout linen thread around it, shaping it all the time by pressing it between your left thumb and forefinger, until at last you have a firm body, smoothly wound, of the same general shape and size as the natural one. When the body is half made you may run the neck-wire through it lengthwise, letting it come out above the centre of the larger end, because the neck is but a continuation of the backbone, which lies at the top of the body. When the wire is inserted, the upper side of the body—the back—must be pinched together and made more narrow than the breast, which is round and full. Be sure that the body is not too large. Better have it too small and too short than too large or long, for the former can be remedied later on by filling out. When the body is finished, bend up the end of the neck wire for an inch and a half at the lower end of the body, enter the point in the lower part of the body and force it down and backward until the end is firmly clinched and will forever remain so, no matter what is done with the other end. Make the neck by wrapping fine, soft tow *smoothly and evenly* around the neck wire from the body upward for the proper distance. Make the false neck a trifle larger than the real one, but no longer. The body is now ready for insertion.

FIG. 49.—Cross Section of Body.

The next step is to take a thread and tie the elbows together, fastening to each humerus just above the elbow-joint. Now take the false body in the right hand, open the skin, introduce the sharp end of the neck-wire into the neck skin, force the wire through the top of the skull in the centre, and push it through until the neck and body come nicely into place. Now see whether the body is of the right size. It should not be so large as to fill the skin precisely, for if so it is too large.

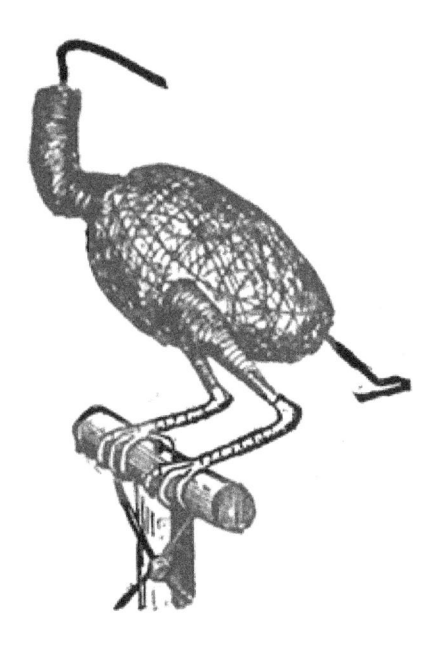

FIG. 50.—The Finished Body and Neck, with Legs in Position.

We must now fasten the legs to the body, and will take the left one first. The leg is still perfectly straight. Hold the lower part firmly between the thumb and finger, grasp the leg-wire, push it on through the leg and enter the sharp point at about the centre of the left side of the false body, and slanting a little forward. (See Fig. 51.) Now push the wire through the body until it projects more than twice the thickness of the body on the right side. Bend the end of the wire until it forms a hook, with the point just touching the body. Now pull the wire back until the point is again forced through and out on the left side for half an inch, which is then bent down and forced firmly into the excelsior, and securely clinched. Wire both legs in this way, and the bird will be so firmly put together it would be almost impossible to pull it asunder.

The legs move freely up and down the leg-wires. Push them up toward the body until the heels are in precisely the same places they were before you skinned the bird—almost hidden in the feathers at a point about opposite the middle of the bird's wing. Now bend the legs forward at a proper angle (see a living bird or a *good* picture) and push some finely cut tow down on each side of the body to fill out the place of the thighs. Insert a little more cut tow, evenly distributed, in the breast, where the crop would properly be, and some more at the base of the tail.

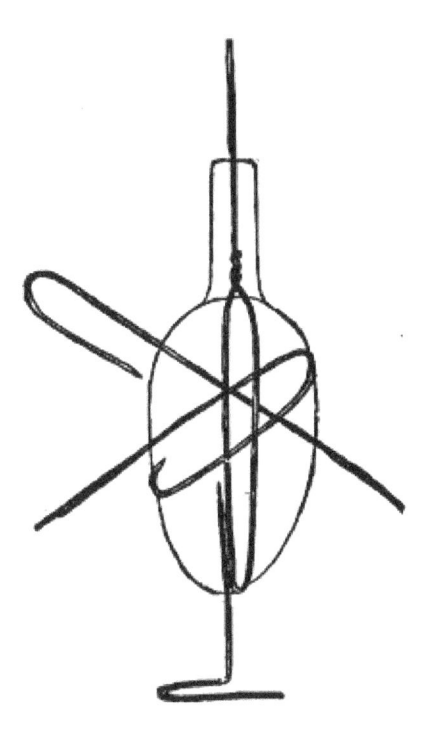

FIG. 51.—How the Leg Wires are Inserted and Clinched in the False Body.

Be sure there are no lumps or wrongly placed masses of chopped tow anywhere in the skin, for if there are any you can not expect to get a smooth and well-shaped bird.

Now take a needle and thread, begin at the upper end of the opening in the bird—on the breast,—and with careful fingers sew the skin together without tearing it or catching the feathers fast. Fill in a little tow, if necessary, as you proceed, but not enough to fill the skin hard and full, and when you reach the lower end of the cut draw the skin of the tail sharply forward for half an inch to take up what it has lengthened by stretching, and sew it fast by several long cross-stitches. At the last moment fill in a little more tow at the base of the tail, sew up the opening, and cut off the thread. The most difficult part of the whole operation is now before us. It now remains to put the specimen on a perch, pin the wings fast to the body, adjust the feathers and wind them down, stuff the head, pin the tail, and put in the eyes.

With a piece of pine board four inches square, and two round pine sticks, each about three inches long, make a rough **T** perch, similar to the one standing vacant on the table in Plate XII. The cross-piece should not be too large for the bird's feet to grasp comfortably. With a small gimlet, or awl, bore two holes in the cross-bar, on a slant, about an inch apart, run the leg-wires through them, perch the bird naturally, and twist the wires together once underneath, to hold it firmly. Study a living bird or a good picture, and give your specimen a correct and natural attitude.

Cut a piece of wire five inches long, sharpen one end, bend it into a **T** shape, as in Fig. 50, and run the sharp end through the base of the tail underneath, and on up into the body. The tail feathers are to rest on and be evenly supported by the cross part at the lower end, which may be either straight or curved, as occasion requires.

With the small forceps, plume and dress the feathers all over the bird, catching them near the root, a bunch at a time, and pulling them into place where necessary. Work them against the grain by lifting them up and letting them fall back into place. It will be a great help if you can at this stage procure a dead bird of the same kind to examine, and see precisely how the feathers lie. One such specimen will aid you more than pages of description.

It often happens that the back, breast, or side of the bird is not quite full enough at some point, or, in other words, is too hollow. Now is the time to remedy such defects. Lift the wing and cut a slit lengthwise in the skin of the body underneath it, and through this opening insert fine clipped tow wherever needed. The forceps is the best instrument to use in doing this. The opening under the wing is *of great importance*, for it gives you command of one entire side of the bird's body. You can by means of this hole fill out the back, breast, or shoulders, if not full enough, and make other important changes in the bird's form. There is no need to sew up the opening when you have finished, for when the wing is pinned in place it will be entirely hidden.

The wings must be fastened to the body before the feathers can be fully adjusted. Cut six small wires, each two inches long, and sharpen at one end. Let us wire the left wing first. Hold it between the left thumb and forefinger, and with the right hand push the point of one of the small wires through the angle of the wing, commonly called the shoulder. When the point is well through, hold the wing in place against the body, adjust it with great care, and when you see that the feathers of the shoulder fall properly over the angle of the wing, push the wire through into the excelsior body until it holds firmly. Push another wire through at the base of the large quills (primaries), and another through the upper part of the wing, just below where it leaves the body. These wires are well shown in Fig. 52. The wing now fits closely against the body, and the feathers fall over it smoothly, so as to completely cover the upper part of it.

Wire the other wing in the same way, taking great care that one is not placed farther ahead than the other, nor farther up or down on the body. The tips of the wings should touch each other exactly at the point. Look at your bird from all sides before finally securing the second wing.

With the wings firmly wired and the feathers nicely adjusted, we next proceed to stuff the head. With the scissors cut up some fine tow or cotton, and by inserting it through the mouth with the forceps, a pinch at a time, fill out around the back and sides of the head, the upper part of the neck and the throat. Do not fill the skin too full, and take care that both sides of the head are precisely the same shape and size. Take plenty of time and do your work nicely.

When the head has been properly filled out, fill in each eye-socket with a little soft clay or putty, insert the glass eyes, and embed them in it. Study the eyes of your dead bird, and imitate their appearance and position with those of your mounted specimen. It is a good plan to put a drop of mucilage around the inside of each eyelid and thus gum it down upon the glass eye. Be sure that the eyes are exactly opposite one another, and that one is not higher nor farther back than the other.

Fasten the mandibles together by thrusting a pin up through the lower mandible into the skull, or else by passing a pin through the upper mandible at the nostrils and tying around the bill behind it with a thread.

It now remains to wind down the feathers with thread to give the bird the exact outline we desire, and to make the feathers lie smoothly. Attend to this with the closest attention and care, for on the success of this process depends the smoothness of your specimen when finished.

The best method of winding ever known is that developed and practised by Mr. F. S. Webster, whose wonderful skill in the treatment of birds is already widely known. His birds are marvels of smoothness and symmetry, and I take great pleasure in describing his method of winding as the best known. First make six hook-wires by filing six pieces of wire, each two inches long, to a sharp point at one end, and bending the other with the pliers in the form of a double hook. (See Fig. 52.) Insert three of these in a line along the middle of the back, and two along the middle of the breast, as seen in the cut. The wing-wires are not to be cut off, but left sticking out for half an inch. The bird is now divided into equal halves, and there are three wing-wires on each side, so that it will not be very difficult to wind both sides alike.

FIG. 52.—The Winding of the Bird.

Now take a spool of white thread, No. 40, fasten the end to the hook-wire on the top of the back; take the base of the pedestal in the left hand and proceed to wind down the feathers. By means of the hook-wires you can wind from point to point at will, so as to bind down the feathers where they lie too high, and skip them entirely where they lie low enough. Get the general outline of the bird first, and apply the thread with a light and skilful touch, so that it will not make creases in the bird. A little practice will enable one to wind a bird with gratifying success.

The next thing is to spread the feathers of the tail evenly, and pin them between two strips of thin card-board placed crosswise to hold the feathers in position until they dry.

Lastly, adjust the toes so that they grasp the perch properly, and set the specimen away to dry where it will not be touched. In about two or three weeks, when it is thoroughly dry, cut the threads off with a pair of scissors, pull out the hook-wires, cut off the projecting ends of the wing-wires close down to the wing, and cut off the wire at the top of the head close down into the feathers.

Mix a little varnish and turpentine together in equal parts, and with a paint-brush paint the feet and bill in case they happen to require it. Clean the eyes and rub them until they shine. You can perch the specimen now permanently on the artificial twig, turned **T** perch, or natural twig, or whatever else you have had in mind. In doing this, clinch the leg-wires together underneath the perch, and cut off the ends so that no portion of the wire will show. Be *neat in everything*, and study to make the bird look alive.

Do not be discouraged if your first bird is a dead failure, nor even if your first dozen birds are fit only for immediate destruction. If you get discouraged because your first attempt at anything is not a complete success, you are not fit to succeed. Better never begin than stop short of success. If you have a love for taxidermy, and the patience and perseverance to back it up, you are bound to succeed.